THE

HARMONY

OF THE

REFORMED CONFESSIONS,

AS RELATED TO THE

PRESENT STATE OF EVANGELICAL THEOLOGY.

An Essay delivered before the General Presbyterian Council at Edinburgh, July 4, 1877.

BY

PHILIP SCHAFF,

Professor of Sacred Literature in the Union Theological Seminary, New York.

TOGETHER WITH THE ACTION OF THE COUNCIL ON CONFESSIONS AND FORMULAS OF SUBSCRIPTION.

Wipf & Stock
PUBLISHERS
Eugene, Oregon

NOTICE.

THE following Essay, or the substance of it, was delivered by appointment in Edinburgh, at the first session of the First General Presbyterian Council, on the Fourth of July, 1877, and led to an action which will direct wide attention to the question of creeds, and bring it before the next General Council, to be held in Philadelphia in 1880. It has been published in England and Scotland, and is now re-published in America, together with the resolutions of the Council thereon, in the hope that it may help to prepare the way for a wise solution of an important and difficult problem of the Reformed Churches.

NEW YORK, Oct., 1877.

Wipf and Stock Publishers
199 W 8th Ave, Suite 3
Eugene, OR 97401

The Harmony of the Reformed Confessions, as Related to the Present State of Evangelical Theology
An Essay Delivered before the General Presbyterian Council at Edinburgh, July 4, 1877
By Schaff, Philip
ISBN: 1-59752-646-0
Publication date 4/14/2006
Previously published by Dodd, Mead & Company, 1877

CONTENTS.

THE HARMONY OF THE REFORMED CONFESSIONS.

THE HARMONY

OF THE

Reformed Confessions,

AS RELATED TO THE

PRESENT STATE OF EVANGELICAL THEOLOGY.

CRANMER'S PROPOSAL OF A REFORMED CONSENSUS.

In the year 1552, while the Council of Trent was framing its decrees against the doctrines of the Reformation, Archbishop Cranmer invited Melanchthon, Bullinger, Bucer, and Calvin to a conference in London, for the purpose of framing an evangelical union creed. To this letter Calvin replied that for such an object he would willingly cross ten seas, and that no labor and pain should be spared to remove, by a scriptural consensus, the distractions among Christians, which he deplored as one of the greatest evils.[1]

In this noble sentiment Calvin expressed the true genius of the Reformed Church, which has always been in favor of union on the basis of truth, and willing to cherish Christian fellowship with other evangelical Churches, notwithstanding minor differences in polity, worship, and even in dogma. Zwingli struck the key-note of this catholic spirit at the conference in Marburg when, with tears in his eyes, he offered the hand of brotherhood to Luther, though he could not agree with him on the mode of Christ's presence in the Eucharist. Calvin once

---

[1] "*Quantum ad me attinet, si quis mei usus fore videbitur, ne decem quidem maria, si opus sit, ob eam rem trajicere pigeat. Si de juvando tantum Angliæ regno ageretur, jam mihi ea satis legitima ratio foret. Nunc cum quæratur gravis et ad Scripturæ normam probe compositus doctorum hominum consensus, quo ecclesiæ procul alioqui dissitæ inter se coalescant, nullis vel laboribus vel molestiis parcere fas mihi esse arbitror. . . . . Mihi utinam par studii ardori suppeteret facultas!*"—See the correspondence in Cranmer's Works (Parker Soc. ed.), vol. ii., pp. 430–433.

declared, that even if Luther should call him a devil, he would still revere and love him as one of the greatest servants of God.

Cranmer, the moderate and cautious reformer and martyr of the Church of England, the chief framer of its Liturgy and Articles of Religion; Melanchthon, "the preceptor of Germany," the gentle companion of the heroic Luther, the author of the Augsburg Confession, and the surviving patriarch of the German Reformation; Bullinger, the friend and successor of Zwingli, the teacher and benefactor of the Marian exiles, and the author of the most œcumenical among the Reformed Confessions; Bucer, the indefatigable, though unsuccessful, peace-maker between the Lutherans and Zwinglians, and the mediator between the Anglican and the Continental Reformation; Calvin, the master-theologian, commentator, legislator, and disciplinarian, who was then just in the prime of his power, and (in the language of John Knox) at the head of "the most flourishing school of Christ since the days of the apostles"

—these representative men, assembled in Lambeth Palace or the Jerusalem Chamber, would have filled an important chapter in church history, and challenged the assent of the Reformed Churches for a common confession of faith that embodied their learning, wisdom, and experience.

But the conference was frustrated by political events, and a Reformed union creed remains a *pium desiderium* to this day. '*Deus habet suas horas et moras.*' It was the will of Providence that the Continental and the English and American branches of the Reformed family should grow up independently, and fulfill their special mission to their age and country. Each shaped its own creed, polity, and worship. Thus, instead of one confession and one catechism which might have answered for all, we have as many confessions and catechisms as there are national Churches, and even more.

THE REFORMED CONFESSIONS.

The Reformed Confessions may be divided into three classes—the ante-Calvinistic or Zwinglian, the Calvinistic, and the post-Calvinistic. The first represent the preparatory stage, and acquired only local authority in Switzerland. The second class were framed under the influence of Calvin's theology after the middle of the sixteenth century, simultaneously with the Tridentine standards of the Roman Church, and in vindication of the protest against Rome. The third class were made in the seventeenth century, and arose from theological controversies within the Reformed Church.

The confessional development of the Lutheran Church began with the Augsburg Confession in 1530, and was completed, after stormy controversies, in the Formula of Concord, 1577. The Roman Catholic system of doctrine received its pyramidal apex only in our age under the long reign of the first infallible pope by the decrees of the Vatican Council (1870). The symbolic tendencies of Romanism and Protestantism are opposite—the former may indefinitely increase the number of dogmas to the maximum of belief, and can never give up or revise a single article without destroying its claim to infallibility; the latter diminishes the number to the scriptural minimum, and allows a correspondingly larger freedom to private judgment and theological progress.

The chief Reformed symbols of the sixteenth century are—The *Gallican Confession*, for the Protestants of France (1559); the *Belgic Confession*, for the Netherlands (1561); the *Second Helvetic Confession*, for Switzerland and other countries (1566); the *Heidelberg Catechism*, for Germany and Holland (1563); the two *Scotch Confessions* (1560 and 1581), which were subsequently superseded by the Westminster standards; and the *Thirty-Nine Articles* of the Church of England (1563), which likewise belong to the Reformed type of doctrine, especially as explained and supplemented by the Lambeth Articles (1595), and the Irish Articles of Archbishop Ussher (1615), which prepared the way for the Westminster Confession.

The two chief symbols of the seventeenth century are the *Canons of the Synod of Dort* (1619), which give the results of the Arminian controversy on the five knotty points of scholastic Calvinism, and the *Westminster Confession* and *Catechisms* (1647), which grew out of the mighty conflict between Puritanism and semi-Romanism, and sum up the results of what may be called the second Reformation of England. They present the ablest, the clearest, and the fullest statement of the Calvinistic system of doctrine. Although least known on the Continent, and given by Niemeyer merely as an appendix to his Collection of Reformed Confessions, the Westminster standards are the most important of the Reformed symbols, and have shown the greatest vitality. It is a remarkable fact that they were made by English divines for three kingdoms under the shade of Westminster Abbey, and around the warm hearth of the historic Jerusalem Chamber, where now the revision of the English Bible is being prepared for the use of all English-speaking Churches. These standards were rejected in the land of their birth, but became the corner-stone of the Churches of Scotland and of Churches beyond the Atlantic and Pacific. Failing in England, they have shaped the theology and religion of countries and nations unknown to the authors. They have been adopted not only by Presbyterians, but also—with some modifications on church polity and the doctrine of baptism, and with a reservation of greater freedom—by the orthodox Congregationalists and the Regular or Calvinistic Baptists in Great Britain and America.

These Reformed Confessions form a very remarkable body of literature. They were composed by confessors and martyrs of the Reformed faith in times of the deepest intellectual and religious commotion, and in the face of cruel persecution. They are fraught with the memories of the most important period of church history, next to the creative period of the apostles. They embody the biblical and theological learning and wisdom of the Reformers, and the ripe fruit of the gigantic struggle with the papal power which had kept the Christian world under discipline and in bondage for many centuries. They set forth, not abstract doctrines, but vital truths for which the confessors were ready to suffer exile, imprisonment, torture, and death. Some are indeed systems of theology rather than popular summaries of faith; but all are full of faith and enthusiasm for the truths of the gospel. They have fashioned the religious opinions and lives of many generations, and trained the most heroic races of Christians and the pioneers of civil and religious freedom—the Huguenots of France, the Burghers of Holland, the Puritans of England, the Covenanters of Scotland, and the Pilgrim Fathers of America. They will ever remain venerable monuments of a pure and heroic faith from the creative period of the evangelical Churches.

The Reformed (as also the Lutheran) Confessions were not intended by their framers to be binding formulas for subscription and checks upon theological progress. Otherwise they would have been made much shorter and simpler. They were originally apologetic documents or vindications of the evangelical faith against misrepresentation and slander. Hence some of them embody a large amount of controversial and metaphysical matter, and are too long and minute for popular use. They resemble the early Christian Apologies, with this difference, that they were directed against Romanism instead of Paganism; and represent a more advanced and mature stage in the development of Christian doctrine. Their official character and their intrinsic merits clothed them gradually with an ecclesiastical authority inferior only to that of the Holy Scriptures. They became the rule of all public teaching in the pulpit and the university. They were a sort of secondary rule of faith (the *norma normata*), derived from the primary rule of the Scriptures (the *norma normans*). They continued in force during the seventeenth and eighteenth centuries, and though since partly displaced in the Churches on the Continent, they still express the faith of some of the most enlightened and active sections of the Christian world.

THE HARMONY OF THE REFORMED CONFESSIONS.

The Reformed Confessions present the same system of Christian doctrine. They are variations of one theme. There is fully as much harmony between them as between the six symbolical books of the Lutheran Church, or between the Tridentine and Vatican decrees of Rome. The difference is confined to minor details, and to the extent to which the Augustinian and Calvinistic principles are carried out; in other words, the difference is theological, not religious, and logical rather than theological.[1]

[1] The documentary proof of this agreement was furnished long ago by extracts from the Confessions them-

The Reformed Confessions are Protestant in bibliology, œcumenical or old catholic in theology and christology, Augustinian in anthropology and the doctrine of predestination, evangelical in soteriology, Calvinistic in ecclesiology and sacramentology, and anti-papal in eschatology.

Let us briefly explain this.

1. Bibliology or the Rule of Faith.—The Reformed symbols unanimously teach, as a fundamental principle of Protestantism, the divine inspiration and absolute and exclusive authority of the canonical Scriptures of the Old and New Testaments in all matters of the Christian faith and morals, in opposition to the Roman Catholic doctrine of ecclesiastical traditions, as a coordinate rule of faith and infallible interpreter of the Scriptures. This doctrine is most clearly and fully set forth in the first chapter of the

---

selves, in the *Harmony of Confessions*, prepared and published under the direction of Beza at Geneva, 1581, in Latin, and translated into English (Cambridge, 1586, also London, 1643 and 1842).

Westminster Confession, which is an acknowledged masterpiece of symbolic statement.

The Lutheran Church and the Anglican Church maintain the same principle, but in practice they allow tradition and the voice of the early fathers and councils a greater authority and influence, especially in matters of church polity and worship, than the Calvinistic Churches.

2. THEOLOGY AND CHRISTOLOGY.—The œcumenical articles of the unity and tripersonality of the Godhead, the incarnation, and the theanthropic constitution of Christ's person, were expressly endorsed by all the Reformers; and hence the Apostles' Creed and the Nicene Creed (to a less extent also the Athanasian Creed so-called) were retained in the Protestant Churches.

Herein the Protestant symbols agree with the orthodox Greek and the Roman Catholic standards in opposition to ancient and modern Trinitarian and Christological heresies. A difference sprung up between the Lutheran and Reformed Christology in connection with the Eucharistic controversy, concerning the extent of the *communicatio idiomatum* and the ubiquity of Christ's body, but this subject belongs to the obscurest corner of theological metaphysics, and does not affect the great truth of God manifest in the flesh, which is taught by both Churches with equal emphasis. The Reformed Christology is more simple and natural than the Lutheran, and accords better with the historical Christ of the Gospels.

3. Anthropology and Soteriology.—The Reformed symbols teach the Augustinian views of sin and grace, that is, the total depravity and condemnation of the whole human race in consequence of Adam's fall, and the absolute sovereignty and sufficiency of divine grace in the work of salvation. They strongly emphasize these doctrines in opposition to the then prevailing Pelagianism of the Latin Church, with its mechanical legalism and meritorious works on which salvation was made to depend. The Reformers passed through the experience of St. Paul; they felt the operation of the law upon the heart and conscience, as a school-

master leading to Christ. They started with an overwhelming sense of the awful fact of sin and the absolute need of redemption. Their theology was intensely practical, and turned on the question, What shall a man do to be saved, and how shall a sinner be justified before a holy and righteous God? To this the New Testament, and especially the Epistles to the Romans and Galatians, returned the answer, Not by any works and institutions of man, not by any outward observances and performances, but solely by the free grace of God in Christ, which is the beginning, the middle, and the end of spiritual life. Thus salvation by grace became the central doctrine, the experimental or subjective principle of Protestantism, and the fountain of comfort and peace in life and in death.

The Reformed system went back to the ultimate source of free salvation in the pre-mundane eternal act of election, upon which the historical process of salvation in all its stages depends; while Luther made the experimental fact of justification by faith alone, the article of the standing or falling Church. The Reformed system, moreover, lays greater stress on holiness and good works, as the necessary manifestation of justifying faith.

In anthropology the Reformers were entirely under the spell of the anti-Pelagian writings of St. Augustine, whom they revered as the greatest, soundest, and most evangelical among the fathers. But his anti-Manichæan and anti-Donatist writings are more on the Roman Catholic than on the Protestant side of the controversy. Zwingli, with his classical rather than mediæval training, was independent of patristic authority, and taught a milder view of hereditary sin and guilt than either Luther or Calvin. The Augustinian system always had some able advocates in the Latin Church, but was overshadowed by hierarchical, sacramentarian, and ascetic tendencies; while the Greek Church adhered to the less definite, we might say, semi-Pelagian views of the older fathers, and lays great stress on the freedom of will.

The Protestant soteriology differs from the

Augustinian, at least in form, and is more evangelical. Augustine, who was poorly acquainted with Greek and Hebrew, and followed the Latin version of the Bible, had the Roman Catholic conception of justification, understanding it to be a gradual process of making just (which virtually identifies it with sanctification); while the Protestant divines, in accordance with the Hellenistic usage of the corresponding Greek terms (*δικαίωσις* and *δικαιόω*) viewed justification as a forensic or declaratory act of acquittal from the guilt and condemnation of sin, on the ground of the merits of Christ, and on condition of faith apprehending Christ, to be necessarily followed by gradual growth in holiness. Justification is the beginning of sanctification, yet distinct rom it as a single act is from a gradual process, as birth is from the life which follows.

4. PREDESTINATION.—The symbols teach the positive decree of an eternal and unchangeable *election* of believers to holiness and salvation, and the perseverance of saints as a necessary means to that end; while the rest are left to the

consequences of their sin. All men are justly condemned, but God in his sovereign mercy chooses to elect a part from this mass of corruption, and to reveal in them the boundless riches of his grace in Christ. This is the amount of the Reformed dogma of predestination as far as it has any practical religious value, and is taught directly or indirectly in all symbols. The negative decree of *reprobation* is wisely passed by, or mentioned only as a judicial act in view of sins actually committed. The fall of Adam is put under a *permissive* (not an *efficient* or *causal*) decree, and the blasphemous doctrine that God is in any sense the author or approver of sin is expressly and emphatically condemned.

This is the infralapsarian scheme of redemption which Augustine taught as a necessary consequence of his doctrine of universal damnation in Adam, and the total moral inability of man. The supralapsarian scheme which differs from the former in the order of the decrees, and, with a severer but terrible logic, represents the fall as a necessary negative condition for the manifestation of God's redeeming mercy on the elect, and his punitive justice on the reprobate, was held as a private opinion by some eminent Calvinists such as Beza, Gomarus, Twiss, but it is not taught in any Confession; even the Canons of Dort, the Westminster Confession, and the Helvetic Consensus Formula, which are most pronounced on the doctrine of decrees, stop within the limits of infralapsarianism. And it should be noticed that the Westminster Confession expressly teaches the freedom of will as well as the sovereignty of God, leaving the solution of the apparent antinomy to scientific theology. It is also a remarkable fact, that in the Westminster Assembly, as the recently published Minutes show, the scheme of a universal offer of salvation or hypothetical universalism found advocates among the ablest and most influential members, such as Calamy, Arrowsmith, Vines, and Seaman.[1]

---

[1] See my work on the *Creeds of Christendom*, vol. i., p. 770.

The subject of predestination holds a prominent, and, we may say, a disproportionate place in the Calvinistic system. It was a necessary and wholesome reaction against the papal doctrine of human merit. It was considered as the backbone of the doctrines of free grace, and was death to all pride and self-righteousness. It furnished an immovable basis in eternity for the salvation in time, and the most solid comfort to the believer, in seasons of despondency and temptation. Hence we find it among all the Reformers. Luther, in his tract on *The Slavery of the Human Will*, which he never recalled, but regarded as one of his best books, goes even further in this direction than Calvin ever did. Melanchthon was at first almost a fatalist (tracing the fall of Adam, the adultery of David, and the treason of Judas to the will of God), but afterwards he suggested what is called the system of synergism (an improved evangelical form of semi-Pelagianism and an anticipation of Arminianism). The Formula of Concord, however, rejected it, and teaches total inability and unconditional election, yet at the same time also universal vocation, or the sincere will of God to save all men, and the resistibility of divine grace.[1] The difference between the Calvinistic and the Lutheran symbols is, that the former are more consistent with the Augustinian anthropology, and give greater prominence to election, while the latter emphasize baptismal grace and a universal call to salvation. But, in point of fact, the vast mass of mankind never hear the sound of the gospel within the limits of the present life to which all orthodox systems confine the possibility of salvation. Calvinism reckons with actual facts as they appear to all observers, and traces them back to the inscruta-

[1] The later Lutheran divines since Hunnius endeavored to solve this contradiction of the Formula of Concord by a distinction between the single *voluntas antecedens* by which God, from eternity foreseeing (not foreordaining) the fall of Adam, resolved to save *all* men, and the double *voluntas consequens* whereby, foreseeing that some would believe and some would not believe, he resolved (likewise from eternity) to save those who would believe, though not *propter fidem*, but *per fidem* or *ex prævisa fide*, and, on the other hand, to condemn those who would not believe.

ble will of God, which is holy and wise, though we cannot fathom it.

5. Ecclesiology.—The Reformed symbols make an important distinction between the visible (actual) Church, which is manifold and exists in various organizations or denominations, and the invisible (ideal) Church, which is one and universal, and embraces all the elect or true believers of whatever denomination or sect. They also distinguish in each visible church or congregation between communicant members which constitute the church proper, and the nominal members or hearers. They lay stress on the necessity of discipline for the preservation of the purity and dignity of the Church. They maintain the right of ecclesiastical self-government, as distinct from the power of the Civil Magistrate; although in practice this right is more or less abridged wherever the Church is united to the State and supported by the State. (For self-government and self-support go together; and he who pays wants to rule.) The Reformed standards teach the parity of minis-

ters, the institution of lay-elders and deacons representing the people, and presbyterial and synodical legislation and administration. The presbyterian form of government was born in Geneva, and fully developed in Holland, Scotland, and the United States.

Herein the Presbyterians differ from Episcopalians on the one hand, who maintain episcopacy and three orders of the ministry, and from Congregationalists on the other, who deny the legislative authority of presbyteries and synods, and teach the independence of each congregation properly constituted according to the Word of God. But the questions of presbytery, episcopacy, and independency are questions of polity, not of dogma. Moreover, the Church of England in her standards holds that episcopacy is not the only, but the best form of government, and necessary not for the being, but only for the well-being of the Church. She never officially denied the validity of non-episcopal orders, and even expressly acknowledged them in various ways down to the period of Laud, the first typical high-churchman, who when he defended the principle of exclusive episcopacy was censured by the authorities of the University of Oxford. The unwise and unrighteous attempts of the Stuarts to force episcopacy upon the reluctant people of Scotland have made the difference much greater than it originally was in the mind of Calvin and Knox, as well as of Cranmer, Latimer, and Ridley.

6. SACRAMENTOLOGY.—The two sacraments of the New Testament are significant sealing ordinances, whose efficacy depends on the faith of the recipient. The *opus operatum* theory, the necessary connection of water baptism with moral regeneration, and all materialistic conceptions of the real presence, whether in the form of transubstantiation or consubstantiation, are rejected.

Here lies the only serious doctrinal difference between the Calvinistic and the Lutheran symbols. The former make spiritual regeneration independent of water baptism, so that it may either precede or succeed it or coincide with it, according to the divine pleasure ; and they teach a spiritual real or dynamic and effective presence of Christ in the Eucharist for believers only, while unworthy communicants receive no more than the consecrated elements to their own judgment. The latter teach unconditional baptismal regeneration, and a corporeal real presence of the true body and blood of Christ in, with, and under the visible elements, for all communicants, worthy or unworthy, though with opposite effects. The Lutheran theory of the real presence and oral manducation requires for its dogmatic support either a perpetual miracle (as the Roman theory of transubstantiation), or the hypothesis of the ubiquity of Christ's body (taught by Luther and the Formula of Concord). This hypothesis is rejected by all branches of the Reformed Church as being inconsistent with the limitation of all corporeal substances, and with the facts of Christ's visible ascension to heaven and future return from heaven. Some of the ablest Lutheran divines, however, sustain on purely philological grounds the Reformed or figurative interpretation of the words of institution, and admit that a literal interpretation of them would lead to transubstantiation rather than consubstantiation.

The Church of England teaches in her formularies the Calvinistic theory of the sacraments in general, and of the Lord's Supper in particular; but in the baptismal service of the Book of Common Prayer she clearly teaches baptismal regeneration without qualification, and in practice she gives larger scope than the Presbyterian Churches to the sacramentarian principle.

7. ESCHATOLOGY.—The Reformed (as well as all other Protestant) symbols recognize but two places and states in the invisible world—heaven for believers and hell for unbelievers, with different degrees of bliss and misery, according to the degrees of holiness and wickedness. They unanimously reject the mediæval fiction of an intervening purgatory for imperfect believers, with its gross superstitions and abuses. The doctrine of the middle state of all departed spi-

rits between death and resurrection, which is distinct from the question of purgatory, was left unsettled, and is to this day a matter of theological speculation rather than positive doctrine. It is characteristic that the scriptural distinction between Sheol or Hades, and Gehenna or Hell, is obliterated in the Lutheran, the English, and other Protestant versions.

THE THEOLOGICAL REVOLUTION.

This body of doctrine laid down in the Confessions maintained its hold upon the Reformed Churches of Switzerland, Germany, France, Holland, England, and America for more than two centuries, and is still a living power in the Presbyterian Churches of the Anglo-Saxon race. It was analyzed, systematized, and developed in all its details by the scholastic theology, which forms a worthy parallel to the mediæval scholasticism of the Latin Church in its relation to the patristic doctrines, being nearly equal to it in metaphysical subtlety, and superior in solid scriptural learning. But all forms of scholasticism are apt to degenerate into a dry and sterile intellectualism, and to provoke a reaction.

After the middle of the eighteenth century, which may be called the century of revolution, a destructive tornado swept over the Churches of the Continent, and threatened to carry away the very foundations of Christianity. It began with Deism in England, which substituted a meager skeleton of natural religion for the revealed religion of the Bible; but the progress of Deism was checked by the Methodist revival, and the apologetic works of Butler and Lardner. In France Deism degenerated into a blasphemous Atheism. Voltaire and Rousseau, the apostles of infidelity and architects of ruin, undermined the foundations of Romanism which, by cruelly persecuting the Huguenots and casting out the Jansenists, provoked the Revolution with its reign of terror. In the Lutheran Church of Germany the negative movement assumed the more serious form of Rationalism which, in its various phases and stages, revolutionized exegetical, historical, and systematic theology. The Reformed Churches of Great Britain and North America, owing to their isolation and their better organization, remained, upon the whole, faithful to their doctrinal and disciplinary standards; but in the Reformed Churches of the Continent the symbolical books were nearly all abolished or reduced to a dead letter, and it seems impossible to restore them to their former authority.

This theological revolution or pseudo-reformation has done, and is still doing, an incalculable amount of harm; but it was a revolt of reason against the tyranny of symbololatry, and proved a wholesome purgatory of orthodoxy. It dispelled old prejudices, and stimulated new and deeper inquiry; it advanced biblical philology and criticism, and enriched the stores of historical knowledge. It compelled the investigation and recognition of the human aspect and fortunes of Christianity in opposition to the exclusive consideration of its unchangeable divine aspect. Thus error is always providentially overruled for the progress of truth.

THE REVIVAL OF EVANGELICAL THEOLOGY.

The nineteenth century may be characterized as the century of revival and reconstruction. Rationalism, indeed, is by no means dead; it continues, in the name of biblical criticism, speculative philosophy, natural science, and humanitarian culture, to undermine the historical foundations of Christianity and all faith in a supernatural revelation; it penetrates the masses by the endless ramifications of the periodical press, which has become a formidable rival of the pulpit. But the antidote is also at hand. An evangelical theology has sprung up which is successfully combating error in all its forms. There is more general intelligence, more vital energy and activity, and a great deal more charity and catholicity in Protestantism than ever before. Bible distribution, home and foreign missions, literary and benevolent institutions are steadily increasing. Germany has taken the lead in the theoretical part of this work of reconstruction, and has been for the last fifty years the chief workshop of evangelical theology, as it has been of Rationalism; while England and America have carried on mainly the practical work of religion, and are above all other nations intrusted with the preservation and spread of Bible Christianity to the ends of the earth. Both are coming nearer and nearer together through their literature and personal intercourse, to their mutual benefit. The Teutonic and the Anglo-Saxon races united are a match for the world. We need not fear the final issue of the present conflict with superstition and infidelity. What the great Athanasius said of the short and abortive reign of Julian the Apostate, may be applied to every phase of error and unbelief: "It is a little cloud, it will soon pass away." Christianity, which has overcome so many foes, and grown stronger in every battle, will no doubt survive; its past is secure, and affords the best guarantee for the future.

THE RELATION OF MODERN EVANGELICAL THEOLOGY TO THE REFORMED CONFESSIONS.

The religious revival of the nineteenth century in the Protestant Churches is a return to the faith of the Reformation as laid down in the Bible and the symbolical books. But it is not a mere restoration of the old, it is also a free reproduction and an advance. The faith is the same, the theology is different.[1] It is different in the form of statement and the relative importance and arrangement of topics. Every age must produce its own theology adapted to its peculiar condition and wants. Thus we have a patristic theology, a scholastic theology, a Reformation theology, and a modern evangel-

[1] [In the discussion which followed, Dr. Begg of Edinburgh took exception to this statement, and said that "all theology was contained in the first promise given in Paradise." To this Dr. Ormiston of New York (himself a native of Scotland, "brought up on oat cakes and the Shorter Catechism") aptly replied : "Very true. In like manner the human race was also contained in Paradise, but it has been wondrously developed since."]

ical theology, not to speak of the various shades of denominational theologies. Divine truth, as revealed in the Scriptures, is unchangeably the same yesterday, to-day, and forever; but it must be ever reproduced, newly appropriated, and represented in all its phases. The human understanding and exposition of the truth is steadily progressing with the Church itself, though passing through many obstructions and reactions. Every true progress in theology is conditioned by a deeper study and understanding of the Word of God, which is ever new, and renewing the Church, and will ever remain the infallible and inexhaustible fountain of revealed truth. The Scriptures may have been studied more intensely and devoutly in former ages, but they were never studied so extensively and with such an array of facilities and advantages as at the present age. Every progress in exegesis must have its effect upon systematic theology and the symbolic statement of truth.

Let us endeavor to indicate the points of

difference between the modern and the old theology of the Reformed Churches as viewed from an œcumenical point of view, and leaving room for some qualifications in detail. Upon the whole the Anglo-American theology is more orthodox in the historical sense than the Continental, but in some points it is more liberal. I have to take an average view before this Assembly which represents all sections of the Reformed Church, and I may be permitted to say that, within the last six months of travel through Europe and the East, I had special opportunities to ascertain the state of theological sentiment on all the leading questions on which I shall touch.

1. Bibliology.—On the fundamental and preliminary question of the divine authority and absolute sovereignty of the canonical Scriptures as the only infallible rule of faith, the position of the Reformed Confessions after an experience of three centuries stands unaltered and impregnable. This is to-day, as it was in the sixteenth century, the *articulus stantis vel ca-*

dentis ecclesiæ evangelicæ, as the article of the divinity of Christ is the *articulus stantis vel cadentis ecclesiæ Christianæ.* "The Bible, the whole Bible, and nothing but the Bible," said Chillingworth, "is the religion of Protestants." Since the development of Vatican Romanism and the rise of Rationalism it is all the more important to maintain our stand upon the immovable rock of God's truth, without additions or deductions. Christ and his gospel are the sum and substance of evangelical Protestantism, as the Church and her traditions are the sum and substance of Roman Catholicism. Protestantism stands or falls with the Bible, Romanism stands or falls with the papacy. We cannot go back to Romanism; still less can we surrender ourselves to the icy embrace of Rationalism. We should, indeed, honor and consult the universal voice of Christendom, and allow it full weight in the interpretation of the Bible; nor should we despise reason, which God has given us as the organ for ascertaining and understanding his revealed truth; but the final appeal must always be to "the Law and the Testimony." Tradition and reason are not the divine Light itself, but, like John the Baptist, they "bear witness of that Light," that "all men through them might believe." *Amicus Calvinus, amicus Lutherus, amicus Augustinus, sed magis amica veritas, et verbum Dei est veritas.*

If the Holy Spirit himself could not clearly and unmistakably point out the way of salvation, it is not likely that popes and councils, composed of sinful and erring mortals, can do it any better. If the teaching of our Lord in the Gospels and Epistles does not contain the pure Christianity, we look in vain for it in the whole domain of ecclesiastical literature.

We must therefore maintain the true infallibility of God's Word against the pretended infallibility of the Vatican, which, like Phariseeism of old, obscures and paralyzes the Bible by human additions ; and against the fallibility of pseudo-Protestant Rationalism, which, like Sadduceeism, mutilates the Bible, and substitutes for it the uncertain guidance of human reason.

The divine authority of the Scripture implies, of course, its divine inspiration, and has no sense without it. But as regards the mode of inspiration, which must be distinguished from the fact of inspiration, the mechanical or magical theory of the seventeenth century, which looked exclusively at the divine aspect of the Bible, and reduced the sacred writers to passive penmen of the Holy Ghost, has been abandoned for an organic theory which does full justice to the human and historical character of the Bible, and regards the authors as the free organs of the Spirit of God, representing the unity and harmony of eternal truth in a variety of gifts and modes of thought and style. The written Word is all divine and all human, and reflects the theanthropic character and glory of the personal Logos who became flesh for our salvation. As the recognition of Christ's full humanity, yet without sin, brings him nearer to us, so the recognition of the human element in the Bible, yet without error, ought to make it clearer to our understanding and dearer to our heart.

This view of inspiration was anticipated by Luther and Calvin, who, with the profoundest reverence for the divine substance of the Bible, had a very liberal view of its human form; it is not inconsistent with the Reformed Confessions, which simply assert the fact of the divine inspiration, without committing themselves to any particular theory of its mode. (The Helvetic Consensus Formula, which teaches even the inspiration of the Hebrew vowel-points, makes an exception, but never acquired general authority.) The Westminster statement on this subject is as cautious and circumspect as it is clear and strong.

2. The Theological Standpoint. — The theology of the Confessions was anti-Romish, and directed against the unscriptural traditions and additions of superstition or misbelief; the modern evangelical theology is anti-rationalistic, and directed against the deductions and ne-

gations of unbelief. The former had to deal with an excessive supernaturalism, the latter with the denial of the supernatural and miraculous. The former was chiefly concerned with anthropological and soteriological problems; the latter has to vindicate the authenticity and integrity of the Bible against negative criticism, the existence and personality of God against Atheism and Pantheism, and the true divinity and historicity of Christ against the mythical, legendary, and humanitarian pseudo-Christologies of the nineteenth century.

Hence some doctrines which were most prominent in the Reformation period must give precedence to others which were then not disputed by the contending parties. Modern theology is neither solifidian nor predestinarian nor sacramentarian, but Christological. The pivotal or central doctrine round which all others cluster, is not justification by faith, nor election and reprobation, nor the mode of the eucharistic presence, but the great mystery of God manifest in the flesh, the divine-human personality and atoning work of our Lord. In this respect modern theology goes back to the primitive confession of Peter (Matt. xvi. 16), and the criterion of John concerning the marks of Antichrist (1 John iv. 2, 3). The great question on which the very existence of Christianity depends is again asked, "Who do men say that I the Son of Man am?" And to this question the experience of eighteen centuries returns the answer of the first confessor, "Thou art the Christ, the Son of the living God."

All evangelical denominations in their ablest divines are verging toward a Christological theology, in which alone they can ultimately adjust their differences. For the nearer they approach Christ, the nearer they will come to each other. Christ is the true concord of ages, the divine harmony of human discords.

3. Catholicity.—The old theology was intensely polemical, denominational, and exclusive. It grew out of the gigantic struggle with the papacy, and in the heat of controversy did great injustice to the mediæval Church, which

after all was the cradle of the Reformation, as Judaism was the cradle of Christianity. The war with Rome was followed by internal wars of equal bitterness between Lutheranism and Calvinism, Calvinism and Arminianism, Episcopacy and Presbytery, Presbytery and Independency. Disproportionate importance was attached to minor points of difference, and the elements of truth on the side of the opponent were ignored or denied.

There is still, and ever will be to the end of the world, a great deal of sectarian bigotry with which even the gods fight in vain, but it has lost its former hold upon the Christian people. The experience of three hundred years, and the vast increase of our knowledge of church history, with its lessons of wisdom and charity, have widened the theological horizon. Denominations which formerly stood in battle array against each other have forgotten their old animosities, and learnt to co-operate freely and heartily in catholic enterprises, and against the common enemies of Christianity.

The articles of agreement are magnified above the articles of disagreement. The Old and New School Presbyterians of the United States, after a thirty years' theological war, have concluded a peace which it is hoped will never be broken, and the result so far has been increased vitality and energy. A similar union has taken place among Presbyterians in England, in Scotland, and in Canada, and will we trust extend still further, until all family feuds of the past shall be healed. The Evangelical Alliance has done much toward individual Christian union, and I trust that the Presbyterian Alliance, while aiming to promote ecclesiastical or confederate union among the branches of the Presbyterian family, will not weaken but strengthen Christian union among believers of every denomination. Both Alliances were chiefly founded and are promoted by the same class of men, and are animated by the same spirit. The problem of Christian union and brotherhood is one of the great problems of the nineteenth century, and will work itself out in various ways until the great prophecy of the one Shepherd and one flock be fully realized.

4. MODERATION OF HIGH CALVINISM.—The scholastic Calvinists of the seventeenth century mounted the alpine heights of eternal decrees with intrepid courage, and revelled in the reverential contemplation of the sovereign majesty of God, which seemed to require the damnation of the great mass of sinners, including untold millions of heathen and infants, for the manifestation of his terrible justice. Inside the circle of the elect all was bright and delightful in the sunshine of infinite mercy, but outside all was darker than midnight. This system of doctrine commands our respect, for it has produced a race of most earnest and heroic Christians, but it is nevertheless austere and repulsive; it glorifies the justice of God above his mercy; it savors more of the Old Testament than of the New, and is better at home on Mount Sinai than on Calvary. "God is love," and love is the only key that can unlock the deepest meaning of his words and works.

The greater liberality of modern Calvinism shows itself especially in the doctrine of predestination and infant salvation.

(*a*) The problem of *predestination* and of the relation of divine sovereignty to human responsibility is not yet solved, either philosophically or theologically, and will perhaps never be solved theoretically until we see face to face. But there is a practical solution in which all true Christians can agree, namely, that all who are saved are saved by the free grace of God without any merit of their own—and this is Calvinism; and that all who are lost are lost by their own guilt in rejecting the gospel sincerely offered to them—and this is Arminianism. Good Calvinists preach like Methodists, as if everything depended on man; good Methodists pray like Calvinists, as if everything depended on God. St. Paul himself represents the fact that *God* works in us both the will and the deed, as the reason why *we* should work out our salvation with fear and trembling. This may be logically inconsistent, but finite logic is not the ultimate standard of infinite truth.

Election by free grace and perseverance of saints (viewed as a duty as well as a divine gift) will no doubt always remain distinctive features of Calvinistic theology, as they are clearly and strongly taught in the Bible, but the decree of reprobation (except as a judicial act for the actual guilt of unbelief) is now rarely taught and never preached. If Presbyterians preach on the mystery of predestination at all, which is very seldom, they never forget to mention human freedom and responsibility, and to trace man's ruin to his own unbelief. No Reformed Synod (at least on the Continent) could now pass the rigorous canons of Dort against Arminianism, which, after a temporary defeat, has silently leavened the National Church of Holland, and which, through the great Methodist revival, has become one of the most powerful converting agencies in Great Britain and America. The five knotty points of Calvinism have lost their point, and have been smoothed off by God's own working in the history of the Church.

(*b*) *Infant salvation.*—It has now become almost an article of faith in the Reformed Churches, that all infants dying in infancy are saved by the atonement.* This is a liberal but entirely legitimate development of the Calvinistic doctrine of election, which allows an indefinite extension of God's saving grace beyond the visible means of grace. All orthodox systems which hold to the necessity of water-baptism for salvation lead to the horrible conclusion that all unbaptized infants dying in infancy, as well as all the heathen, that is, by far the greatest part of the human race past and present, are lost forever. It is a poor relief if Augustine, who first clearly taught this unchristian dogma, makes a distinction between negative damnation or absence of bliss, and

* As far as America is concerned, Dr. Hodge positively affirms that "he never saw a Calvinistic theologian who held the doctrine of infant damnation in any sense." See his *System Theology*, vol. iii., p. 605, and my work on *Creeds*, vol. i., p. 795.

positive damnation or actual torment, and assigns to infants "the easiest room in hell." Hell is hell, and was made only for impenitent sinners who refuse to be saved. Zwingli was the first, but the only one among the Reformers (except his friend and successor, Bullinger), who had the courage to oppose this dismal view, and to teach the salvation of all infants, and of a large number of adult heathen. The second Scotch Confession "abhors and detests," among the doctrines of the Roman Antichrist, "his cruel judgment against infants departing without the sacrament." The Westminster Confession teaches that "elect infants dying in infancy, and all other elect persons who are incapable of being outwardly called by the ministry of the word, are regenerated and saved by Christ through the Spirit, who worketh when, and where, and how he pleaseth." It is true some of the older Calvinists make a distinction between elect and reprobate infants; but the Calvinistic system allows the charitable assumption that all infants dying in infancy are among the elect, and that their removal from a world of temptation before committing any actual transgression and contracting personal guilt, is a proof of God's saving mercy to them. There can be no salvation without Christ, but salvation does not necessarily require a historical knowledge of Christ any more than damnation requires a historical knowledge of Adam's fall. It is the *will* of our blessed Saviour, who took special delight in children, that "*none* of these little ones should perish."

5. Religious Liberty.—The Calvinistic (as well as the Lutheran) Confessions presuppose a Christian State and a uniformity of belief among the people, and assign to the Civil Magistrate the duty not only to support the Church and its ministry, but also to punish heresy as an offense against society. The principle and practice of persecution for religious convictions prevailed almost universally since the days of Constantine and the union of Church and State, although the persecuted party always

complained of the application, on the ground of innocency. In the age of the Reformation the Anabaptists and Socinians were the only Christians who advocated toleration from principle. The burning of Servetus for heresy and blasphemy is the one dark stain on the fair fame of the great and good Calvin, but it was justified even by the gentle Melanchthon. Anabaptists were drowned and burnt by the score in Protestant as well as Roman Catholic countries. The Church history of England from Henry VIII. down to William III. is an unbroken tragedy of persecution of Romanists against Protestants, Protestants against Romanists, Anglicans against Puritans, and Puritans against Anglicans. Even the virgin soil of New England was stained by the martyr blood of Quakers, under the theocratic rule of Congregationalism, whose champions in the Westminster Assembly had advocated the sacred rights of conscience. All Protestant sects, with the exception of a few which never had a chance to rule, are guilty of intolerance and persecution, though in a far less degree than the Roman Church, from which they inherited the principle, and which adheres to it to this day, as the Papal Syllabus of 1864, and the Pope's recent conduct in Spain abundantly prove.

The Act of Toleration in 1689, though far from the full conception of the rights of conscience, closes the dark chapter of religious persecution in England, at least under its more violent form, and inaugurated the era of religious liberty among Protestants. The Baptists and Quakers made the doctrine of religious liberty an article of their creed. By a combination of various causes it has become almost a universal belief among Protestants, at least in Great Britain and in North America, that God alone is Lord of the conscience, that faith is a free act which cannot be enforced, that all coercion in religious matters is evil, and evil only, and contrary to the teaching and example of Christ and his apostles. Spiritual errors must be spiritually judged by ecclesiastical censures, admonition, suspension, and excommunication. The Civil Magistrate has no control over heresies and schisms, and is bound to protect the liberty of conscience and of public worship as one of the fundamental and inalienable rights of all its citizens, so far as this liberty does not interfere with the peace of society.

On this subject the Anglo-Saxon Protestants are ahead of the Continental Protestants. In the United States the Episcopal Church has changed the Thirty-nine Articles, and the Presbyterian Church the Westminster Standards, so as to adapt them to this modern conviction; while in England and Scotland the objectionable clauses have become a dead letter, or are expressly disowned, or liberally explained. The battles of Christendom must hereafter be fought out on the basis of freedom and equality before the law, and without those carnal weapons which are forbidden by the spirit of the New Testament.

THE REFORMED CONSENSUS AND THE PRESBYTERIAN ALLIANCE.

This is, I trust, a fair historical statement of the Consensus of the Reformed Confessions, and the present state of Evangelical theology in relation to it.

We now approach the difficult and delicate practical question of the relation of this Alliance to the Consensus. The constitution adopted in the preliminary meeting at London (21st July, 1875) lays down as the doctrinal basis of the Alliance, "the Consensus of the Reformed Confessions." But it does not define this consensus, nor is there any recognized formula of the kind. The subject, therefore, will have to be settled sooner or later, and this is the proper time to discuss it, although we may not be prepared to take any definite action. I shall confine myself to a few suggestions which I offer with modesty and some diffidence to the consideration of wiser heads.

To avoid misunderstanding, and perhaps unnecessary apprehension, I must remark at the outset, that the question before us is not the question of the revision of the Westminster Confession, or of any other confession. That must be left with the particular Church or Churches which own that confession. This General Presbyterian Council, moreover has no jurisdiction or legislative authority. It may indeed define its relation to the historical confessions, or set forth a new one, but it would have no binding force upon any Churches except by their own act of adopting it.

We may state our relation to the Consensus in two ways—the one negative, the other positive.

1. The doctrinal consensus need not be formulated at all, but may be left an open question, which every delegate must decide for himself. The Council may trust the personal character of the individual members, as a living guarantee for the doctrinal purity and soundness of the body. The Christian faith is older than

the Apostles' Creed, and the evangelical faith is older than the Protestant Confessions. Sooner or later questions as to the precise nature and extent of the Consensus will probably spring up; but it is not necessary to anticipate future difficulties.

2. The doctrinal consensus can be formulated by the Presbyterian Council after long and mature deliberation. This again may be done in three ways—

(*a*) By a list of doctrines, or an index of the chief heads of doctrine on which agreement is desired and required as a condition of membership, without defining the doctrines themselves. There can be no doubt that the Reformed Confessions teach the same views on the divine inspiration and authority of the Scriptures, the unity and tripersonality of the Godhead, the divine-human constitution of Christ's person, the atonement by his blood, election and salvation by free grace, justification by faith, the Church and the sacraments. Such a list would be similar to the Nine Articles of the Evangelical Alliance. The prevailing theology might show itself in the order and the wording of the articles. But it would be merely a skeleton of a confession.

(*b*) A historical statement, or brief summary of the common doctrines of the old confessions, without additions or changes. Such a summary has been actually prepared for this Council by my friend, Dr. Krafft, professor of Church History in the University of Bonn, who is thoroughly familiar with the confessions, and in sympathy with their spirit. His paper would form a good basis for an official document of the Council, if it should deem proper to adopt this course.

(*c*) A new œcumenical Reformed Confession. By this I mean the Consensus of the old Reformed Confessions freely reproduced and adapted to the present state of the Church; in other words, the creed of the Reformation translated into the theology of the nineteenth century, with a protest against modern Romanism and Rationalism. This would be a work for our age, such as Cranmer invited the Reformers to prepare for their age, and would thus fulfill the joint wish of these great and good men.

A new confession would be a testimony of the living faith of the Church, and a bond of union among the different branches of the Reformed family, as the Apostles' Creed is among all Christians, or as the common English version of the Scriptures is among English-speaking Protestants. It would not necessarily interfere with the provincial authority of the numerous confessions over which this Council has no control, and with which it ought not to meddle. It would have to be prepared by a body of able, wise, and godly divines, representing all the Churches of the Presbyterian Alliance, for *quod tangit omnes debet tractari ab omnibus.* Its authority would of course depend upon the general consent of the Churches.

The preparation of such a confession would afford an excellent opportunity to simplify and popularize the Reformed system of doctrine, to utter a protest against the peculiar errors and dangers of our age, and to exhibit the fraternal attitude of this Alliance to the other evangelical Churches which have sprung up since the Reformation and have been blessed by God. It ought to be truly evangelical catholic in spirit. A confession which would intensify Presbyterianism and loosen the ties which unite us to the other branches of Christ's kingdom, I would regard as a calamity. We want a wall to keep off the wolves, but not a fence to divide the sheep; we want a declaration of union, not a platform of disunion.

The right to frame a new confession or to revise the old ones is beyond dispute. The desirableness of a common doctrinal bond of union among the Reformed Churches is likewise apparent. But the expediency of such a work at the present time is, to say the least, very doubtful. The pear may be ripening, but it is not ripe yet. If we were ready for it, I would say, let us take this course, but we are not prepared for it. Let me state the reasons.

In the first place, creeds and confessions of faith which have vitality and power, usually spring from great doctrinal controversies and deep religious commotions. They cannot be made to order, like political platforms. No amount of theological learning and literary ability is sufficient. They require a religious fervor and enthusiasm that is ready for any sacrifice, even the death of martyrdom. They are solemn acts of faith, and the product of a higher inspiration.

In the second place, our theology is in a transition state, and has not yet reached such clear and definite results as could be embodied in a form of sound words. It would be impossible to unite all the Reformed Churches under an elaborate theological confession such as were those of the sixteenth and seventeenth centuries. The new Form of Concord might become a Form of Discord. The Anglo-American Churches would require a maximum of orthodoxy, the Continental Churches would be content with a minimum of orthodoxy. The recent Continental confessions framed by the Free Church of the Canton de Vaud, 1847 (thirty printed lines), the Free Church of Geneva, 1848 (seventeen articles, one hundred lines), the General Synod of the Reformed Church of France, 1872 (fifteen lines), of the Evangelical Church Association of Switzerland, 1871 (twenty-two lines), of the Free Church of Italy, 1872 (eight articles, thirty-eight lines), of the Free Church of Neuchatel in 1874 (a dozen lines), are very brief, and leave room for a great variety of views.[1] So are the Nine Articles of the Evangelical Alliance.

---

[1] We give as a specimen the Confession of the "Evangelical Church of Neuchatel, independent of the State," which is as follows :—"Faithful to the holy truth which the apostles preached, and which the reformers brought again to light, the Evangelical Church of Neuchatel acknowledges as the source and only rule of its faith the Holy Scriptures of the Old and New Testaments. It proclaims with all the Christian Church the great facts of salvation, condensed in the Creed called the Apostles' Creed. It believes in God the Father, who has saved us by the life, death, and resurrection of Jesus Christ, His only Son,

It seems to me, therefore, that the most we can do in the present Council is to intrust this whole subject to the hands of an able and comprehensive Committee, with instructions to gather all the necessary information about creeds and subscription to creeds within the bounds of this Alliance, and to report thereon to the next triennial meeting.

One word in conclusion. A creed is a response of man to the questions of God; but God's Word is better than the best human creed. A creed is a confession of faith, but faith is better than the confession of it, and without faith the best confession is but "as sounding brass or a tinkling cymbal." Much as we esteem doctrinal unity, there is a higher unity, the unity of spiritual life, the unity of faith, the

---

our only Lord; and who has regenerated us by the Holy Spirit. And it confesses this faith in celebrating, according to the institution of the Lord, the sacraments of Baptism and the Lord's Supper." The new French Confession, which is similar to this, see in my work on *Creeds*, vol. i., p. 500; the Geneva Confession, in vol. iii., p. 781; the Free Italian Confession, in vol. iii., p. 789.

unity of love which binds us to Christ, and to all who love him, of whatever denomination or creed. Let us, with Peter and Thomas, confess Christ first and Christ last, and let our confession be an act of worship, an act of personal and collective self-consecration to him who saved us from sin and death, and leads us to immortality and glory. Let us not forget what the most logical and the most theological of all inspired apostles says, that now we see through a glass darkly, but then we shall see face to face; that now we know in part, but then we shall know in full, even as we are known.

"And now abideth faith, hope, love, these three; but the greatest of these is love."

ACTION OF THE GENERAL PRESBYTERIAN COUNCIL ON CONFESSIONS OF FAITH.

The Author of the preceding essay was followed by his friend, Prof. J. Godet, D.D., of Neuchatel, who addressed the Council in eloquent and elegant French on the importance of making the eternal divinity of our Lord and Saviour the burden of our confession, in opposition to modern infidelity (comp. p. 43). The Rev. Alex. Cusin, of Edinburgh, read a translation of a formulated Consensus of the Reformed Confessions, in thirty brief articles, which Prof. W. Krafft, D.D., of Bonn, had prepared for the Council. Then followed an interesting discussion on the subject of Creeds, in which Drs. Brown of Aberdeen, Lang of Glasgow, Tulloch and Mitchell of St. Andrews, Begg of Edinburgh, Candlish of Glasgow, Pressensé of Paris, and others, took part.

At the close of the discussion, Alex. Taylor Innes, Esq., of Edinburgh (the author of a standard work on *The Law of Creeds in Scotland*), offered a series of resolutions, which were seconded by Chancellor Howard Crosby, D.D., of New York; referred to the Business Committee; reported back by Dr. Calderwood, in the name of that committee, on the next day (July 5), "as competent under the Constitution of the Council," and unanimously passed as follows:

"That this Council appoint a committee with instructions to prepare a report to be laid before the next General Council, showing in point of fact—

"*First,* What are the existing creeds or confessions of Churches composing this Alliance? and, What have been their previous creeds and confessions, with any modification of these, and the dates and occasions of the same, from the Reformation to the present day?

"*Second,* What are the existing formulas of subscription, if any, and what have been the previous formulas of subscription, used in these Churches in connection with their creeds and confessions?

"*Third,* How far has individual adherence to these creeds by subscription or otherwise been required from the ministers, elders, or other office-bearers respectively, and also from the private members of the same?

"And the Council authorize the committee to correspond with members of the several Churches throughout the world who may be able to give information, and they enjoin the committee, in submitting their report, not to accompany it either with any comparative estimate of these creeds and regulations, or with any critical remarks upon their respective value, expediency, or efficiency." [1]

At a later meeting, on motion of the Business Committee, the following gentlemen were appointed a committee on Creeds and Formulas of subscription under the above re-

---

[1] The restriction of the Committee to mere facts was no doubt intended by the mover to cut off opposition and to secure a unanimous vote.

solutions: Dr. Schaff, New York (Convener); Professor Mitchell, St. Andrews; Professor Candlish, Glasgow; Professor Calderwood, Edinburgh; Professor Lorimer, London; Dr. Knox, Belfast; Professor Jean Monod, Montauban; M. De Pressensé, D.D., Paris; Professor Godet, D.D., Neuchatel; Professor Bulogh, Debreczin; Signor Charbonnier, Italy; Pastor Cisar, Nove Mento, Moravia; Dr. Alex. A. Hodge, Princeton, U. S.; Rev. G. D. Mathews, New York; Dr. Brown, Richmond; Dr. Peltz, New Paltz, N.Y.; Dr. Cooper, Alleghany; Dr. Stewart Robinson, Louisville; Principal Snodgrass, Kingston, Canada; Dr. Topp, Toronto, Canada; Rev. A. Campbell, Geelong, Australia; Messrs. George Junkin, Philadelphia; James Mitchell, LL.D., Glasgow; A. Taylor Innes, Esq., Edinburgh; and David Laing, LL.D., Edinburgh.[1]

ACTION OF THE COMMITTEE.

This Committee, at a meeting held during the Sessions of the Council, took the following action, as recorded by its secretary, Mr. Innes:

"At a meeting of the Committee of the General Presbyterian Council of 1877, appointed to prepare a report to the next Council on Confessions and Formulas, held in the College rooms of the Free Church of Scotland, on Monday the 9th July, 1877,

---

[1] Four members were added afterwards, see p. 69, footnote.

Dr. Schaff was called to the chair, as Convener.

Mr. Taylor Innes was appointed to act as clerk to the meeting.

It was resolved that the work of the Committee be done as much as possible by the facts called for in the Remit being ascertained for each country by the members of Committee belonging to that country, under charge of the following Conveners:

For Scotland, Prof. Mitchell.

" England, Dr. Lorimer.

" Ireland, Dr. Knox.

" British Colonies, Dr. Snodgrass and Mr. Campbell.

Dr. Lorimer to act as general Convener.

For the Southern States, Dr. William Brown.

" " Northern States, Dr. A. A. Hodge and Rev. G. D. Mathews.

For the Dutch Reformed Church, Dr. Peltz.

Rev. Mr. Mathews to act as general Convener.

For Holland, Dr. Hoedemaker (to be added to Committee).*

For France, Prof. Monod.

" French Switzerland, Prof. Godet.

" German Switzerland, Pastor Bernard (to be added to Committee).*

For Bohemia and Moravia, Mr. Cisar.

" Hungary, Prof. Balogh.

" Italy, Mr. Charbonnier.

" South Africa, Rev. Mr. Murray (to be added to Committee).*

---

* MM. Hoedemaker, Bernard, and Murray, with the Rev. Owen Thomas of Liverpool, were next day (10th July, 1877), added by the Council to the Committee originally appointed.

Prof. Monod of Montauban to act as general Convener.

It was also resolved that the returns be as far as possible digested in each country by the Conveners and general Conveners, and that the results, with as much of the materials and documents as may be necessary, be transmitted through these general Conveners to Dr. Schaff [Bible House, New York], so as to be in his hands not later than the 1st of January, 1879.

It was resolved that while the older and larger creeds already found in collections need not be printed except in so far as necessary to understand the modifications of them, all such modifications, with their dates and occasions, and all formulas of adherence since the reformation, be printed. And Dr. Schaff was authorized to apply to any committee having charge of funds with a view to next Council or on behalf of the Alliance, for such funds as may be necessary to meet the expenses.

Mr. Innes was instructed to write to the members of Committee, and especially the Conveners, intimating generally the resolutions of the meeting.

(Signed,) PHILIP SCHAFF,
Chairman.

A True Copy.
ALEX. TAYLOR INNES,
Secretary."

www.ingramcontent.com/pod-product-compliance
Lightning Source LLC
LaVergne TN
LVHW012334100826
845148LV00017B/2560

* 9 7 8 1 5 9 7 5 2 6 4 6 3 *